Center Your Thoughts

JUST WRITE

Align Your Spirit

Published by True Beginnings Publishing. Copyright by Shanovia Lumpkin, 2020.

Just Write—Center Your Thoughts, Align Your Spirit, by Shanovia Lumpkin. © Copyright 2020. All Rights Reserved and Preserved. No part of this book may be reproduced or transmitted in any form or by any means, electronic or mechanical, including photocopying, recording, or by information storage and retrieval systems or other electronic or mechanical methods, without written permission of the Author with exceptions as to brief quotes, references, articles, reviews and certain other noncommercial uses permitted by copyright law. For permission requests, write to the Publisher, addressed "Attention: Permissions," at the address below.

true_beginnings_publishing@yahoo.com

Formatting, Editing, and all artwork by True Beginnings Publishing. All Illustrations, Cover Art, and text are Copyright Protected.

ISBN-13: 978-1-947082-10-6

Ordering Information:
To order additional copies of this book, please visit Amazon.

This book is a compilation of affirmations by the Author to facilitate journaling. All quotes, thoughts, and writings are products of the Author's imagination. Any resemblance to actual events or persons, living or dead, is entirely coincidental. The quotes, thoughts, and writings are copyrighted to the Author and are protected under US Copyright law. Any theft of the Author's work will be prosecuted to the full extent of the law.

Just Write—Center Your Thoughts, Align Your Spirit.
© Shanovia Lumpkin.
First Printing, 2020.

This journal is a dedication to those who want to master the art of self-control and be better than yesterday.

"I want to grow. I want to be better. You Grow. We all grow. We're made to grow. You either evolve or you disappear."
~Tupac

Instructions

Write as if your life depended on it.
Be honest and transparent with yourself to receive the best results.

Introduction

Some of us hide behind forced smiles, most of us are not okay, and many of us are at war with the thoughts in our heads. Mental illness, depression, stress, anxiety, and PTSD can be the determining factor of life or death. Harboring all of these thoughts and feelings inside is as if being a land mine hidden in the field life—one wrong step and BOOM—life, as we know it, will be destroyed/over. This journal is here to serve as your dumping ground, your words of reason, and your safe space; a therapeutic tool for organized venting and self-improvement. This is your journal therapy.

What is therapy? Per Google, "Therapy, also called psychotherapy or counseling, is the process of meeting with a **therapist** to resolve problematic behaviors, beliefs, feelings, relationship issues, and/or somatic responses (sensations in the body)." Though this is the ideal way to go, sometimes the best results come from helping oneself. So, do it! Help yourself. Just Write!

There is something so amazing about peace of mind. It is as if you breathe easier and deeper. You sleep more comfortably and relaxed. You think logically and with precision. Find your peace, protect your energy, live, and be happy. **Q:** What is your definition of peace? What steps can you take to protect your energy? Are you living or merely existing? On a scale of 1-10, how happy are you? Today, I Affirm:

God always provides a way out. Nothing is too overwhelming for God. He can do anything but fail. Relax. **Q:** Think of a time when you were in distress. It seemed as if you had exhausted all of your options and you had no clue what you were going to do. Then boom! A miracle happened or things began to align in your favor? Take this time to name seven blessings, and when you are done, write "Thank you" in all caps because that is the magnitude of your gratitude. Today, I Affirm:

In life, things happen; some beyond our control and others because of poor decisions. Either way, you control the way you react. Do not be the one who overreacts and acts out irrationally. Moreover, do not be the one who has a meltdown and folds under pressure. Take a deep breath, channel your emotions, and think before you speak. A calm spirit and relaxed mind can configure a promising solution and positive results. **Q:** Are you temperamental? How well do you handle stress under pressure? Do you think before you react? Before making a decision, what steps do you take to ensure it is the best decision? Are you a problem-solver or a person who gives up? Today, I Affirm:

Even the ones who always have it all together have moments where they fall apart. It is hard being strong all the time. Sometimes you just need a break. That load gets real heavy some days, and you can feel yourself losing control. Your patience is thin, your anxiety is high, and you are super agitated; literally a ticking time bomb ready to explode. In addition, it is hard trying to keep your composure when it feels like everything is falling apart. You need a break; a mental and physical vacation to get away from it all. Just a moment of silence and peace to relax, regroup, and refocus. **Q:** Do you have a superhero complex? Are you the one who saves everyone? How often do others check in on you? How often can you ask the favors that others ask of you? When was the last time you pampered yourself? When was the last time you took a mental health day? Today, I Affirm:

Rid your mind of malicious thoughts and ill intent. Manifest peace and happiness. Calm your spirit and radiate a relaxing aura. Let nothing and no one disturb your peace. **Q:** List seven things that weigh heavy on your spirit. Underneath that list write: "I release myself of this burden. I free myself of these thoughts. I will no longer allow this hurt to taint my spirit and stunt my growth." Today, I Affirm:

If it is not making you better as an individual, building your business, supporting your endeavors, or putting money in your pocket, then it is wasting your time, draining your energy, and distracting you from your purpose. Do not feel bad for wanting more for your life. You deserve financial stability. You deserve happiness. You deserve peace. In addition, if anyone comes around disturbing those treasures for you, either eliminate it or minimize access to you. **Q:** On a scale of 1-10, how focused are you? Do you surround yourself with like minds? Can you build with your circle? Do you have a support system? How often do you finish what you start? Are you prepared to walk away from anything that does not contribute to your happiness and growth? Today, I Affirm:

You have to protect your energy and your peace. Their energy may be toxic and can transfer right to you, and vice versa. **Q:** Do you have a toxic spirit? Are your thoughts pure? How often do you evaluate your circle? What energy does each individual bring to your life? Are you in need of a cleanse? Today, I Affirm:

_____
_____
_____
_____
_____
_____
_____
_____
_____
_____
_____
_____
_____
_____
_____
_____
_____
_____
_____
_____
_____
_____
_____
_____

DO NOT let the toxic words, insecure spirits, and the envious, jealous thoughts of unhappy humans deter you from your money or your gift. Be cautious, moving forward. There are individuals that depend on your energy and need you in tiptop shape. When you allow people to steal your joy, it also steals the joy of those that need you the most. **Q:** On a scale of 1-10, how affected are you by the words, thoughts, and opinions of others? Do any of these words, thoughts, and opinions finance, feed, or bring you intimate pleasure? Now make a list of how these words, thoughts, and opinions are beneficial to your life. Multiply that by 0 and that is how much you should care. Today, I Affirm:

Deal with that suppressed anger, rage, and depression. If you do not, it will lead to your demise.
Q: What makes you angry? How often do you feel rage? Depression comes in many forms. How often do you find yourself wanting to sleep more than you prefer to be awake? When are you most anxious and agitated? Can you talk about issues, problems, and emotions without raising your voice or using obscenities? Do you listen to comprehend and understand? On the other hand, do you listen to rebuttal and object? Can you agree to disagree? Alternatively, do you prefer to be always right? Are you open to compromise? Are you willing to find common ground? Do you feel compromising is forcing you to conform? Are you afraid of change? Today, I Affirm:

WHEN ONE IS MENTALLY EXHAUSTED, THEY BECOME PHYSICALLY TIRED AND DRAINED, WHICH LEADS TO EITHER SLEEP DEPRIVATION OR COMPLETE HIBERNATION. **Q:** Are you someone who lays awake at night because your thoughts will not allow you to rest? Are you someone who feels the only time you can be at peace is when you are asleep? Did you know mediation brings peace and clarity to one's mind? Did you know Yoga has poses to clear a cluttered mind? Here are a few poses you can try: Mountain Pose, Warrior I, Warrior II, Warrior III, Butterfly Pose, Savasana. Today, I Affirm:

Feed your mind. Feed your soul. Read! **Q:** Did you know reading reduces stress and fights against depression symptoms? When was the last time you read a book? Below, I have listed great reads for your mental pleasure.

- *Dear Young Kings and Queens*, by Shanovia Lumpkin
- *Align*, by Shanovia Lumpkin
- *Priceless Treasures*, by Shanovia Lumpkin
- *Backpack Prophet*, by CJ Farquharson
- *Broken Heals*, by Tiffany Young
- *Dear God Hear My Prayers*, by Lakisha Johnson
- *Destined To Succeed*, by E.M. Sweeting

Today, I Affirm:

"Life is a gift! Appreciate it. Do not take it for granted. Do not waste it away. Do not ruin it. Build yourself upon a solid foundation. Never get complacent in your situation. Always want more and better for yourself. Believe in your ability to be great. You are greatness in its rarest form. You are amazing in every aspect of the word. You are you! So be the best you that you are destined to be." **Q:** In what ways do you show appreciation to yourself? Do you believe in yourself? On a scale of 1-10, how often do you compliment yourself? I would like you to encourage and speak life into yourself today. List seven characteristics that identify with your character. Start each sentence with "I Am" (example: I am selfless, a creator, a visionary etc.) Brag on yourself for what makes you great! Today, I Affirm:

Do not entertain ignorance, just eliminate communication and cut ties. Keep your sanity and protect your peace. Remember, it takes two to argue, so do not waste your breath. **Q:** Are you argumentative? Is your spirit easily disturbed? In the heat of the moment, can you keep your composure? Are you capable of having a conversation or discussion without lashing out at the other person's response? Can you be the calm spirit and leveled head in the midst of turmoil? Can you speak and keep a mellow tone when you are upset? Are you willing to remove yourself from any situation that threatens your sanity and peace? Today, I Affirm:

Be happy! Continue to be patient. Always remain humble. Eliminate the stress. Treat people the way you want to be treated. Consistently pray and be thankful. Surround yourself in positive energy. Love with no caution. Give whole-heartedly. In addition, live peacefully. Remember, you are one of God's genuine blessings in its rarest form. **Q:** Are you happy? What is your definition of happiness? What makes you happy? What is your happiness based on (example: people, places, or things)? List seven things that make you happy and why you cannot function without each one. Today, I Affirm:

RELEASE

Who I was then is not who I am now. Every day, I work toward a better me, one day at a time.
Q: What type of the person were you in the past? Describe the person you are presently. Are your wants and needs the same from then and now? Have your changes made you better? Describe the person you aspire to be in the future. What steps are you taking to be the person you aspire to be? How do you handle the reminders from others of your past self and lifestyle? Today, I Affirm:

Holding your thoughts and opinions hostage can often turn into the fuel used to start an enormous emotional fire. Do not explode or self-destruct over time due to the lack of communication. Respectfully speak your truth, allowing the opportunity for rectification, explanation, or separation. **Q:** On a scale of 1-10, how well do you communicate? When things are bothering, are you confident in addressing them? Are you comfortable expressing yourself? What makes communicating hard for you? What is your biggest pet peeve when communicating? What is your biggest fear when trying to communicate? How can you communicate better? Today, I Affirm:

So many of us bury burdens of scars that we thought we healed from until something triggers it. I pray that God helps you to grow past your pain to the point that it disappears in the rearview mirror of your life, never to be seen again. I pray that it never resurfaces to hunt you in your dreams, present, or your future. Release yourself, free yourself, because YOU ARE DELIVERED. In Jesus' name I pray, Amen. **Q:** Are you aware of what triggers you? Have you healed from the traumas you do not voice? Have you forgiven yourself for the things you allowed to bring you pain? Have you learned from your past mistakes? Are you moving forward or still repeating the cycle? Are you living in the now or revisiting the past? Do you need help to transition past this hurt? Have you ever thought about seeking professional council? Did you know by dialing 211, you could access resources and referrals in your community for personal crisis and everyday needs? Today, I Affirm:

Let go and let God. Release the hurt, disappointment, shame, and resentment. Understand that as long as you hold onto it, you are hurting yourself. Free your mind, body, and spirit. Once you do this, only then will you truly be able to live and be happy. **Q:** Let us have a lemon squeeze. Take this time to scream, yell, cry, and write it out. Who has hurt you? What is hurting you? When did this happen? Where did this happen? Why are you hurting? What can you do to move forward? Today, I Affirm:

Give love to others that you wish to receive. Be patient with others as you would like them to be patient with you. Be kind to others as you would want them to be kind to you. Respect others as you would want them to respect you. Release any resentful feelings that you may carry in your heart and mind. Disburse of them before they find a permanent home in your spirit. Be mindful and considerate of your behavior, the seen and unseen. Always display honorable characteristics. Be humble enough to know when to sit your pride to the side. Be selfless, calm, and forgiving. Let your aura radiate good and positive energy. Be respectfully truthful. Trust others as if you have never experienced a lie. Protect as if your livelihood depends on it. Hope like a child who still has their innocence. Moreover, persevere no matter what. You may stumble, even fall, but you will always rise again. **Q:** Do you believe the energy you release into the universe will determine your blessings? Do you know what it means to empathize for someone other than yourself? On a scale of 1-10, how patient are you? Do you treat others the way you want to be treated, or do you treat them how they treat you? Do you believe matching energies will result into beneficial solutions? Are you being a reflection of what you would like to see in the world? Today, I Affirm:

It is never a good idea to go to bed mad. Make your peace with things you have no control over. In addition, work diligently on the areas that you can improve. Release anything negative that has a hold on you so that you can genuinely have eternal peace. **Q:** Are you someone that dwells on disappointments? Do you allow those feelings and emotions to marinate in your spirit? Do you find yourself having dreams that reflect your emotions? Do you wake up restless, tired, and still thinking about the night before? If the issue is resolvable, talk about it calmly and find a solution before bed. If not, agree to disagree and let it got. Meditating on things beyond our control is insanity and can cause you to react irrationally. Make peace with your emotions or simply release them back into the universe. Nevertheless, no matter what, choose to remain in control. Today, I Affirm:

There is something so unique about a sense of peace, relief, and release. When one feels heavy, isolated, and numb, it takes a toll on not only the body but also the mind and spirit. Today is the day you will let it all go. It is time to forgive. Hope and believe that all will be all right. You will not give up; you will not be defeated; you will continue to press your way through. **Q:** What do you do to relieve stress? Have you ever gotten a massage? Did you know soaking in a warm bath or listening to soothing music can relax your mind? Have you ever practiced mindful meditation or breathing exercises for relaxation? All of these things can help with aligning your spirit and centering your thoughts. Today, I Affirm:

RESOLVE

In order to solve a problem, a solution must be found. One can find a solution by dealing with the difficult situations. A solution is found by coming to a mutual agreement. **Q:** Are you a problem solver? How do you respond when faced with a difficult situation? How often do you come to a mutual agreement in moments of turmoil? Today, I Affirm:

Stop venting about problems and start finding solutions. **Q:** Are you a frequent venter? When problems or issues arise, do you phone a friend or family member? On a scale of 1-10, how often do you do this? Does phoning a friend or family member resolve your problems or add fuel to the fire? Have you ever tried Googling solutions to the issue at hand? Did you know stress and anxiety are transferrable? This means you can transfer your energy to the next person or household. Are you okay with making your family and friends your dumping ground for your heavy loads? Are you considerate of others? Do you transfer good energy? Does your good energy outweigh the negative energy? I know there are some situations where mediation is the best solution, but it is not required all the time. Thinking before reacting can eliminate the need to include others. Today, I Affirm:

You have to shake this depression, anxiety, and "fuck it" spirit. Do not allow yourself to be easily defeated. You are a warrior, not a worrier. Snap out of this funk and start fighting for the life you want. **Q:** Are you a person with a long list of wants? Do you blame others for the life you have lived? Do you take responsibility for your actions? Do you know what it means to be accountable? Are you or have you ever been in a funk? How long does your funks usually last? What are you doing daily to regain your momentum? Do you know what a vision board is? Have you ever created a vision board? Do you own a dry erase board? Did you know when you write your goals, see your goals, and make steps to attain your goals, you can attain them? Do not make excuses or throw pity parties. Get up and make things happen! Today, I Affirm:

Positive thoughts equal positive results. Manifest it mentally from within as you work on it in the physical realm. In addition, it shall happen. With faith the size of a mustard seed, watered with hard work and love, it will be yours. **Q:** What are you doing daily to reach your goals? Are you aware that every effort counts toward your ultimate goal? On a scale of 1-10, how patient are you? How positive are your thoughts as you go through the process to your success? Do you complain a lot? Are you willing to build the foundation brick by brick? Understand that nothing worth having will come easy. You have to put in the work. Today, I Affirm:

I pray that God calms your spirit, sharpens your focus, guides your thoughts, and orders your steps. Trust everything is going to be all right. **Q:** Are your thoughts, spirit, and emotions all over the place? Do you feel off at times because life seems to be chaotic and unclear? Do you know keeping a writing journal can help with this? Sometimes, in order to find the solution and make sense of the problem, it needs to be visual in black and white so one can decipher what seems to be the unknown. Write in down in the journal and figure it out? Today, I Affirm:

Practice discipline and self-control. We all have areas in our lives that we would like to improve, decrease, or even start. Strategize and focus. I have learned that nothing happens overnight, which is why I take everything one day at a time; speaking aloud is a form of affirmation and confirmation. **Q:** Are there areas in your life that require some intimate attention? Finish the statements: I need to improve… I need to decrease… I need to start…Today, I Affirm:

Do not be easily angered. The person that has the power to ignite your rage is a person who can control your energy and alter your mood. Unbothered is the new wave. Ride the tide of peace. **Q:** How often do you allow the actions of others to alter your mood? In what ways does it affect you? What can you do to minimize your reaction? Today, I Affirm:

RENEW

Forgive so that you may live in peace. Let go of all the memories or feelings dwelling inside that are corrupting your soul. Release and let God create in you a clean heart and a renewed spirit. **Q:** Do you know how to co-exist peacefully? Is it hard for you to let go? Did you know in order to forgive one must cease blame towards others and focus on understanding oneself? What will it take you to move on? How often do you go to sleep angry? Today, I Affirm:

I pray that God rectifies, heals, and restores any and everything in your life that needs to be renewed. I speak peace, progress, and promotion over your occupation. I ask that God enlarges your territory. In Jesus' name I pray, Amen. **Q:** What do you need to correct? What do you need healed? What do you need restored? What do you need renewed? Say this aloud: "I speak peace, progress, and promotion over My Life. I ask that God enlarge My territory. In Jesus' name I pray, Amen." Today, I Affirm:

Focus on the reflection in the mirror. Let nothing and no one deter you from your progress. Thank God you do not look like what you have gone through. Praise him for always keeping you, even when you fall short. Pray for your strength, mentally, physically, spiritually, and emotionally. Be thankful for your growth, no matter how enormous or minute. You are not the same; you have changed and are evolving every day. Pray God grants you eternal peace to live without a care in the world and be unbothered, unshaken, and unmoved by the tricks of the enemy. In Jesus' name I pray, Amen. **Q:** When you look in the mirror, what do you see? Write this and say it aloud: "I believe this prayer. I will receive these blessings. I claim this prayer, declare, and decree this prayer shall come to manifestation." Today, I Affirm:

_____
_____
_____
_____
_____
_____
_____
_____
_____
_____
_____
_____
_____
_____
_____
_____
_____
_____
_____
_____
_____
_____
_____
_____
_____

This is your season of transition. It may not be what you want or feel that you need at this moment in time, but it may be what you need. Continue to be steadfast and focused. Pray your way through. Press your way through. You are almost there. **Q:** Did you know to transition one must be ready for change? How do you handle sporadic change? Can you adapt easily or are you stuck in your ways? Today, I Affirm:

Some things you just cannot do anything about. Most things are beyond your control. So focus on what you can do and what you can change. Emphasize on being the best you God created you to be. Be the vision and example of what you want to see. **Q:** On a scale of 1-10, how often, do you worry about things beyond your control? What does your energy reflect? When you come around, are you welcomed? If you expired today, what would be your legacy? Are there some changes that need to be made for a better and brighter future? Today, I Affirm:

I will no longer allow things beyond my control to stress me. I will focus on the things I can change and ignore the things I cannot change. In addition, I will focus on the progression of me. Elevation is my sole purpose. **Q:** On a scale of 1-10, how much do you love yourself? Do you love yourself enough to live for you? Do you know the Serenity Prayer? How can you be better than yesterday? Today, I Affirm:

History is exactly that! Do not live in the past. Instead, focus on your future. The future is so much better and brighter. **Q:** Have you ever done a "Burn Notice?" A burn notice is evicting anything in your life that brings you pain, despair, anxiety, depression, and stress. You get an index card or sheet of paper and list everything that fits in the categories. Say a prayer of release and relief; prayer for the strength to continue moving forward and never going back. Finally, you burn it. Yes, set it on fire! Ashes to ashes, dust to dust. The objective of this exercise is to be stronger and wiser going forth. Today, I Affirm:

God built you to stand. You may bend, but you will never break. You are strong, and you will always be victorious. Speak light, breathe life, and spread love. You have the power to manifest everything that your heart desires. Tap into your strength and leave behind an unforgettable legacy.

Q: On a scale of 1-10, do your good days outweigh your bad? Do your blessings outweigh your shortcomings? How many times has your life been spared from thoughtless and irresponsible decisions? How many times have miracles happened when it seemed like you were out of options? Do you see how blessed you are? Today, I Affirm:

Trying to find one's way back to wholeness is not always an easy task, as it is a continuous work in progress. One has to cleanse their surroundings, mind, body, and spirit, with the understanding that the blame cannot be placed on others, but it's the reflection of oneself. One's isolation is not always personal towards others, but it is a process when one is trying to heal and rebuild. **Q:** SELF-REFLECTION: Who are you? I forgive myself for the following. List below. SELF-AWARENESS: What do you need to change? I forgive others for the following. List. CHANGED ENVIRONMENT: What steps do you need to take to execute those changes? Are you moving accordingly? Today, I Affirm:

Positive thoughts equal positive results. Manifest mental healing, financial growth, and peace of mind. You possess the gift of gab. You have the power to speak positive change and transition. You are so much stronger than you give yourself credit. **Q:** Do you know how Dope you are? Are you aware of how powerful your thoughts and words are? Are you mindful of your words and thoughts? Are you ready to receive that which you seek? Today, I Affirm:

Declare that today will be a good day. Get up, get out, and be proactive as well as productive!
Q: Make a "To Do" list. List everything you would like to accomplish today. Cross each one out as you complete it. It is okay if you did not get everything done, but feel accomplished by the tasks you did fulfill. Today, I Affirm:

Sometimes you have to be selfish in order to focus and accomplish your goals. Distractions slow you down and make it hard to stay on track. I am learning what is meant for you will be, regardless. Your success is beneficial to everyone in connection to you. The loyal will understand and support, opposed to everyone else who will complain and make excuses. **Q:** Do you know how to be selfish of one's self and time when you are on a mission to manifest your vision? Are you easily distracted? Do you believe your blessings will be yours? Circle, check: Who supports you? Who is not praising your wins? Did you know sarcasm is a form of disdain? Are you paying attention? Today, I Affirm:

Do not lose focus. Do not get distracted. Stick to the plan. Remember, that which you wish to accomplish takes discipline. You got this. See you at the finish line. **Q:** Victory speech time!! Yes, write this speech as a confirmation of your vision becoming a reality. Write the details of how you remained focused, the distractions you eliminated, the sacrifices you made, how sticking to your plan was beneficial, and why. Then, sign it! Your John Handcock is very important and represents your stamp as well as confirmation of your manifestation. Today, I Affirm:

God, clear the smoke screen from my life. Give me 20/20 vision and the strength to stay focused on the bigger picture, along with the patience and endurance to see it through. Sometimes, it is difficult for one to see what we need when we are so fixated on what we want, what feels good, and what looks good. One does not realize they are being derailed from their life's purpose. Distractions come in many shapes, sizes, and forms. Do not miss out on your blessings because you refuse to let go of your lessons. **Q:** It can be hard to be honest with oneself when it means sacrificing something you love, think you need, or are comfortable with. Moment of truth, are you living up to your full potential? Do you play more than you work? Is there something or someone you are keeping around because of convenience and comfort? Do you need to remove something or someone who is not bringing substance? Today, I Affirm:

RESTORE

To restore, one must bring back something that may be broken, reinstating power that may have been lost when trying to please others. Alternatively, it could have been lost due to insecurities, fear, and lack of motivation. Nevertheless, on this day it is time to take your power back! **Q:** What are you lacking? What has been broken and needs restoration? What steps can you take to gain it back? Today, I Affirm:

"It's a new year! A new day that was not guaranteed but was given and granted. Be thankful you made it because some did not. Take this opportunity to say thank you. Make a plan and execute the great things you would like to accomplish going forward. Leave the past where it is and just focus on the future." **Q:** Every day, one should set at minimum seven things you would like to accomplish for that day. List your Seven Tasks that you would like to complete below. Set a deadline and time you would like to have everything done. Did you complete everything? If not, that is okay. Your effort was appreciated. Moreover, if you are blessed to see tomorrow, take advantage of that opportunity to work toward all you wish to achieve in this lifetime. Today, I Affirm:

In due time, everything will work itself out. Just pray and not worry. What God has for you is for you. Moreover, what is meant to be will be. Just stay true to thyself. Focus on the better of you because what you put out is what you should receive in the end. **Q:** Have you ever thought of your life as a garden? A good location, growing a variety of plants, and a planned layout is like your thoughts on a vision board. Gathering seeds, plants, supplies and equipment is like gathering all the information needed to manifest caring for the soil, and planting the seed is your investments. Keeping down weeds and controlling the pests is damage control, staying clear of distraction and negative energy. Watering and harvesting at quality peak is determination and enjoying the fruits of your labor. Today, I Affirm:

Distractions are lethal weapons used to slow you down. When you are focused on your vision, let nothing and no one deter you from what you wish to achieve. **Q:** Do you know how to focus? How mindful are you? Are you good at managing your time? Have you ever heard of the Pomodoro Technique? Fun fact, The Pomodoro Technique is a timer to break down work into 25-minute intervals and short breaks. Today, I Affirm:

Never let the weight of this world deter you from life's happiness. Always remember there is light at the end of the tunnel. You just have to have a plan. Stay focused and execute it. **Q:** Understand that you are not alone. In life, we live through many experiences. Did you catch the key word in that sentence? Live! Write what you are living through: I am living through... Now rewrite it beginning the statement with: I survived... This is you speaking victory over your life's circumstance. Today, I Affirm:

_____
_____
_____
_____
_____
_____
_____
_____
_____
_____
_____
_____
_____
_____
_____
_____
_____
_____
_____
_____
_____
_____
_____
_____

The time is now to envision and set goals. Create a plan. Map out every step. Stay focused and stick to it. Do not get sidetracked. Moreover, always remember to live life for you. **Q:** How vital is your vision to you? Are you confident in its manifestation? How close are you to fruition? Will you give up? Today, I Affirm.

Hope is only a fraction of what is required to achieve greatness. Through prayer, meditation, and effort, you can achieve any goal no matter the magnitude. Continue to have tunnel vision and focus on completion. **Q:** Are you known for your optimism? Do you set unrealistic expectations for yourself? Does your effort match or exceed your expectations? How often do you make excuses? Are you vibrating an energy of completion? Today, I Affirm:

REGROUP

In order to regroup, one must reassemble their lives, which means some things may have to be adjourned and put back together. In order to rebuild and be better, dismantling may be required. Remove the parts that no longer work, are not a good fit, or no longer serve a purpose. **Q:** Is dismantling and rebuilding a challenge for you? Are you open to change? List seven things that need to be removed from your life. How soon can you make the necessary adjustments? Today, I Affirm:

Suppose something is taking all of your energy to the point that you would rather be asleep than awake. Suppose you would rather be at work than at home. If you feel like every time you indulge in its presence, you are aggravated, agitated, and overwhelmed, save yourself the stress, stroke, and anxiety. Let us not live in the realm of depression. Release so you can find peace. Holding on only causes more damage. Positive vibes only. If it does not make you better, it should hold no relevance in your life. **Q:** How often do you focus on yourself? How do you replenish your energy? How often do you neglect yourself? Do you have a void you are trying to fill? Do you know your worth? Do you believe you deserve genuine love and happiness? Do you believe that some things happen for our own good? Did you know the benefits of healing oneself is more gratifying than expecting this from others? Today, I Affirm:

Redirect your focus and expand your vision. Other people's success is not your come up. There is nothing like your own. **Q:** Are you more concerned with the progress of others, opposed to focusing on your own? Are you closed-minded? Do you believe in yourself? Do you feel entitled to other people's benefits? What do you have going for yourself at this time? How can you perfect and elevate your own situation? Today, I Affirm:

Be thankful that you do not look like your trials and tribulations. Your life is a testimony. Every breath is a new opportunity. Progress is your focus—one day at a time. **Q:** Take a moment to reflect on the many obstacles you have overcome. Today, I Affirm:

Because you are faithful and focused, you will be victorious. Everything you are working for and towards will be yours. **Q:** Do you see your progress? Are you proud of yourself? What can you do to be better than yesterday? Today, I Affirm:

This is the year of progress and increase. We will no longer be the tail but embrace our rightful place as the head. We will no longer be the borrowers because the blessings God has set up for us; we will be able to be the lenders. We will not allow our past hurt, indiscretions, shortcomings, or fear keep us captive in the mindset of complacency. We have forgiven others for their indiscretions and asked for the forgiveness of our own. This is our new start. This is the year that we set goals and accomplish them. We lead this year by example. This is the year of fulfillment and completion. Train your focus to remain the focus. You have no time for irrelevant distractions. Only accept good vibes that contribute to your growth: spiritual, mental, physical, and emotional. I speak unending prosperity, peace, love, and happiness over your life from this day and always. **Q:** How would you do the same for yourself? Today, I Affirm:

Be proactive today. Write a list of things you wish to accomplish and stick to it. This will require discipline and focus. Do not deter from what you wish to complete. **Q:** What tasks did you complete today? Today, I Affirm:

REFOCUS

Refocusing requires adjustments. Adjustments require alterations. In addition, alterations are made through action and processing. Many want to change but do not to make the necessary adjustments required to do so. **Q:** When was the last time you did a self-evaluation? Were you happy with the results? Did you see areas of concern? Are you ready to make the necessary adjustments? What do you need to change first? Today, I Affirm:

Utilize your wit in every situation. Make intelligent decisions. Speak less, listen more, and stay focused. In addition, you can obtain everything your heart desires. **Q:** How often do you think before you react? Do you weigh the pros and cons of your reactions? Did you know that there are brain exercises you could implement for mental strength? Did you know jigsaw puzzles, cards, dancing, or even tai chi is exercises to keep you mentally sharp? Today, I Affirm:

Speak these words aloud: I am learning to have a manifesting state of mind. From my finances, to happiness, and peace, I am learning to speak life into every situation my family, my businesses, and my circle of friends. I am trying to build a community of positive likeminded individuals whose focus is to be better than yesterday. **Q:** Do you have a manifesting state of mind? Do you utilize your words to shape your life? Do you believe in the words you have just spoke over your life? Today, I Affirm:

"Slow and steady is still in motion." Trust the process, build, and progress. New Year, same vision, more focused, and fewer distractions. Manifest everything your heart desires. **Q:** What progresses have you made this week? Are you satisfied with your accomplishments? Are there times you want to give up? What keeps you going? Today, I Affirm:

Shift your energy, redirect your focus, and manifest your vision. **Q:** On a scale of 1-10, how positive is your energy? Do you need to detox or cleanse your spirit? What is your focus? Are there obstacles or distractions slowing down your progress? Do you believe you can achieve anything you set in your mind to accomplish? Today, I Affirm:

Stay focused on the goal at hand. Believe in yourself. Be a balance of confidence, humility, and a hint of a savage. Listen to comprehend and execute with precision. Keep calm at all times. Control your emotions. It is not over until it is over. I believe in you. I am rooting for you. You got this!

Q: Do you believe in yourself? On a scale of 1-10, how confident are you? Are you humble? What level is your comprehension: beginner, intermediate, or advanced? Are you open and receptive to learning? Are you mentally prepared to adjust and change in order to elevate? Are you ready to take control of your life? Today, I Affirm:

If one is not active, they get bored. When one becomes bored, they are not motivated. Without motivation, one is not productive. Without productivity, one is easily distracted and loses their way. Thought of the day: Redirect your focus and get back on task. **Q:** How often are you bored? On a scale of 1-10, how motivated are you? Are you proactive daily? Are you easily distracted? Are you ready to transfigure your life? Today, I Affirm:

TRANSFORMATION

You control the energy you allow in your space.
Protect your peace.
Monitor your circle.
Eliminate all negativity.
Think positive.
Be positive.
Live in peace.
Every decision you make shapes or breaks the progress you desire.
Make your next move your best move.
I believe in you, but I also need you to believe in yourself.

#peace
#positiveenergy
#selfevaluation

~About The Author~

Shanovia Lumpkin, also known as Priceless Treasure, is a freelance writer born and raised in Miami Florida where she learned the value of an education at a very young age. Shanovia developed a keen interest in expressive writing, which became evident in the eloquence of her poetry.

It was then that Priceless Treasure found her inner strength and self-awareness that propelled her into a life of abundance through vigilant affirmations and prayer.

"Priceless Treasures" is her first published book.

You can also find the Author in these places:

~**Instagram**~
_pricelesstreasures

~**Twitter**~
@PricelessT21588

~**Tumblr**~
priceless-treasures.tumblr.com

~**Facebook**~
www.facebook.com/AuthorPricelessTreasures/

www.ingramcontent.com/pod-product-compliance
Lightning Source LLC
Chambersburg PA
CBHW080449110426
42743CB00016B/3324